I0750289

FINISHING LINE PRESS
www.finishinglinepress.com

Diary of an Intercessor

poems by

Kay Bell

Finishing Line Press
Georgetown, Kentucky

Diary of an Intercessor

ISBN 978-1-64662-391-4 First Edition

ACKNOWLEDGMENTS

Black or Brown first appeared in Moko Caribbean Arts and Letters, July 2016 Issue 9

Before You Were My Child (for Micah) first appeared in Mothers Always Write, July 2016

Constructing a Dream (for Zaire) first appeared in the Voices Project, June 2017

For Kalief, We Are Loners (for my brother), & Untitled 5 first appeared in The Write Launch, September 2017

Privacy is an edited version of the poem first published by PRONG & POSY Fall 2017

And first appeared in the free Library of the Internet Void, June 2018

Wait (for Us) first appeared in the Rascal Journal, September 2018

Truth first appeared in Pithead Chapel, October 2019

Publisher: Leah Huete de Maines
Editor: Christen Kincaid
Cover Art: Photo by Mona Eendra on Unsplash
Author Photo: Kay Bell
Cover Design: Elizabeth Maines McCleavy

Order online: www.finishinglinepress.com
also available on amazon.com

Author inquiries and mail orders:
Finishing Line Press
P. O. Box 1626
Georgetown, Kentucky 40324
U. S. A.

Table of Contents

Valley of Dry Bones

Ode to My Ancestors

I looked for someone among them who would build up the wall and stand before me in the gap on behalf of the land so I would not have to destroy it, but I found no one.

Ezekiel 22:30

Bronx Hymns

For Kalief

a book bag; universally colored, tucked inside an orange jumpsuit, arranged as a jacket to metal doors, and bed bugs chained to delinquents. The souls of hungry men, guilty or innocent, are built together with frantic eyes, caught on the edge of paper-thin cots,

kill beat kill.

This is the day lonely eyes are seized, ensnared on an island in a room intangible but authentic with blueblack feelings and disarmed manhood on suicide watch.

I take the #42 bus to BCC and wonder if we have ever smoothed the edges of our faces against books and noise.

I know you.

You are tongues of sanity, urban sidewalks littered with segregation and televisions that avoid speaking our truths. You are mangled atrocities, an unchecked mailbox, a registered voter, left in a facility of shame. And as I pray, I can't hold you, I can't capture your beginnings.

A book bag, an orange jumpsuit, a language of injustice, a memory of valor. Be still now and

sleep.

Before You Were My Child

for Micah

Before you were my child
heaven draped you across my womb.
Your anatomy was copied,
from two imperfect beings
and became a deep crease,
bent in the middle of
a full-size mattress.

You were curved like your
grandmother's back,
as you rolled your sentiments into me,
inhale by exhale, by inhale,
and I exhaled a field of poems
and expressive masterpieces
into your laughter, your eyes,
the birthmark on your bottom.

You were a sky then.
Coarse coils of curls and Caribbean roots,
your movements jerked-
like Sunday's chicken.

my "woody"
my "bambino"

you were always mine.

Before you were my child,
you belonged to your father,
and his father's philosophy of soundless
performances.
You sat in my womb,
as an open door;
your movement was your only speech.

You were the breeze that snuck in
between the strands of my hair,
the thin threads of gray on your daddy's chest,
a mirage of olive trees
I have always wanted to plant.

You were the tears rolling down the
face of your ancestors,
and a meadow of cactuses,
shaped like a guitar,

And when you untied yourself
from the cord that held us together,
you traveled
across an overextended passage,
above a beating heart,
smooth and sweet;
a cloud wrapped in a velvety blanket,
pulling on my breast
commanding daybreak...

Song of Boaz

you're the reason why I came

to be absorbed in a hallowed space
to glean in a poetic field
to leave what's dead   for the dead
to keep the things that can't be scorched
to be a Saturday revolution:

where the world is our domain
& every lyric is a sun

to be reminded of the latter
to widow regret
to black this body with your arrows
to love it   to love on it

to offer a ritual of masterpiece
to name desire   in its throbbing
to land the heart
where the seedlings dwell
to find something naked
and breathing

to abyss the famine of our beginnings

you're the reason why I stay

Prayer I

you knitted me/ in a womb/of fire and brass/and the thunder/of my womanhood/is your mouth   opening wide/baring trumpets/in a whispered roar/resurrecting dry bones/and fallen men/who cannot wreck/these plans/ you have for me/that sometimes/I cannot comprehend/but as you mold my clay; fragile; innocence/I embrace wind, love and tears/and thank you for what is whole/in breath and dust/in blood and covenant/and with a heart/full of your word/that I may not sin/ against thee/a heart mounted/on eagle wings/ after sleep/in the branch of a vine/such an unearthed space/that makes me/ fruitful/adored/empowered/justified

We are Loners

for my brother

You told mommy you hated her today,
but I knew
that was a lie.
You held that Heineken bottle tightly,
like your nephew
clinging to his favorite blanket.
Your sturdy hands were shaking and I witnessed the privacy of your afflictions
in your dialect
and sweaty forehead.

There is a story to tell,
I promise one day I will tell the world that all the odds were against you
and that Barbados raised you alone.
I will not leave out the flawlessness of your swaying body
against Kartel tunes
or the cod fish and rice with lentils
in the winter.
The liability isn't all yours.

I know the pain rides you.
But we are loners, brother.
We live in a land where we must "honor thy mother and thy father"
or we won't live long enough to see our tears trace the city like bridges.
There are no morals to your story,
only a restricted beginning
forging an appetite for women
and children
with hostilities.

But, you are not the "Prodigal Son"
you are a father and brother,
rising before day
to iron your clothes
and begin your hustle,

because "the early bird catches the worm"
and you are destined to fly above lifeless expectations
speaking the language of the stars.
You were never an illusion, or fiasco,
you have not failed.

When you spoke to mommy today,
those lies didn't bandage my revelations.
You wanted to be held,
for real.
but instead,

you drank your Heineken and sat down.
Mommy sobbed in the corner
and I smoked a cigarette at the table,
as our sister was yelling something about telling you to leave,
while our children were asleep in the back room.

Who will tell your story?

There are Bajan dreams dying
on the inside of a man.
There are remnants of his nightmares
stirring his nostalgic sorrows.
Marijuana stained secrets
relating to his
insensible one-night stands
and there are people walking by,
doing nothing…

We are loners, brother.
We rip the flesh off bones of truth;
There are hills in our backs and jungles in our souls.
We walk on frayed ankles,
born as Bajan pariahs
and American misfits;
we scream quietly.

We know no mothers
or fathers
or the love that comes in between.

No one understands us.

I sung a black girl's song today,
but tomorrow
I vow,
I will tell your story.

Symptoms of Peter

Because your mouth
is intentional, passionate &aimlessly labored
towards impulse and rebellion.

Because you slaughtered a soldier's ear
that night we got drunk and tore
the petals off the roses.

Because my lipstick is smeared
along the road
we travelled for Pepsi's, sandwiches and solace.

Because the rooster crowed
and we both heard it—
clinging to Jersey sheets.

Because love is a sacrifice
that knew we would betray it

Because we are both thorned, awkward, and transformational:
falling over the edge of the boat

Because neither of us can swim

Constructing a Dream (an ode for Zaire)

You take the cereal boxes away from their fate
and you fill them with purpose;
they come alive as trains, elevators, sometimes an emotional mother

and as a city is built in your youth and virtue
you seize its possibilities; taking all the risks
to inspire an old moon to harvest great beginnings

I carried you once, 4 pounds of growing belly
my heart burned, and I was alone
but not really

You stroked my maternal odds and made me something
each time I tried to convince myself
I was better off dead

Now, I buy the family size boxes of cereal, the ones with extra room
for seats and passengers who bear sons of their own;
sons who are faithful to the occupation of unconditional love

and because I am so clumsy and sensitive
I often crush the corner of the rectangular packages
before I get them home

You say: "Momma, I will use it anyway"
and I cry in private
as you go in your room and build us both a dream.

Psalm for My Mother

I am your daughter
sprawled across your belly,
          kissing the love that grips you,
grasping the aching of suns,
 heaving the journey
of what has been
          splintered & kidnapped,
from the voice
that no longer belongs to you.

Praise the days
for their length
          and the nights,   for hidden joy,
and for the little girl
          inside of us both
that no one has touched
          or shaped   by the acid of tears
& the shrinking of bones.

The little girls
 who know   today
          cannot be yesterday
& we must embrace tomorrow: alive
in the menacing joy of our   history…

Untitled 9

For this lust,
rocking me tonight,
catching each drop of sweat.
This amused
little something,
giving me unease
in the apprehensive purple;
front seat of your mind,
perfume stampeding the air:
"te quiero ahora"
we are collectibles,
evading the dust,
in this small place,
this earthypalace,
this funroom, this foreign exchange
where there are always scars:
"hold me papi,"
rock the sweat of summer in my thighs,
sway this shit.
"Baila dentro de mi"
Let the world see us
this way.
Lust for what makes you victorious,
Lust for what makes you swim,
Lust for what's full and ripe.
Keep rocking.

Wait (for Us)

Until the butter softens on the toast
Until the doorbell rings and it's a package that needs a signature
Until we are books and our pages are dust
Until the shower runs long enough to steam the mirror
Until the cat lurches on the sofa; hungry, needy, human
Until the curtains aren't hiding our blemishes
Until we are in repose but nothing's happening
Until our feet are warm
Until we are bleeding truth
Until the paint is peeling off the walls
Until we begin to laugh again
Until we are water, dancing into ice cubes
Until we are poetry
Until we know the stars will come
Until the chaos has made us one
Until we are invisible
Until,

we're in the middle of the living room
and the earth is now our flesh...

Bronx Hymn

Was there a garden or was the garden a dream? —Jorge Luis Borges

after Harlem,
it was you,
and the fractured walkways
where people desperately aspired
and played Bachata
and made the concrete *home*

&

where clothes hung
from windows
and the metro was booming
& where God rang His music
from the church on top the Hill.

&

where the weeds were in remorse
and paradise was a portrait
it was you
in the rubble of creation
on Ryer & Washington Ave.
barely a hum in a fetching memory
scarcely a gaze of yellow glory

it was you gone.

Burning Bush

Ark of Covenant

In every song
          we are obedient
you teach me to master curry
and I teach you the anatomy
          of the poem

but that never stops them
          from touching us

they give us secrets
          we bear   in American children

we drown in fire   we are prey

          insert Moses

He tiptoes down   the mountain
bearing the stone of law
   and it's breaking

he protects it within an Ark.

The rock cries out
because our flesh are idols
and we have become   renegades

but thou shall not murder
                    the hands that ripened you

                    &
thou shall not   forget the lust
          or mercy
or how many times you said "No."

          And now,
          in every song   we sing about a box
                    covered in gold.

Its contents   a symbol of our bodies.
We seal the box shut. They pry it open.
They drown in fire.
We watch them burn.

The Woman with the Issue of Blood

Tell them
        you're not innocent.
That your story   is not home
and you're drowning
        in the blood
flowing
        from your river
        of red sin.
                Tell them.
You gave me away
until I was   raw and bruised
and couldn't recognize
        myself.
        Tell them   you're not sorry
        and now your insides
        are sinking:
        in spaces   where you find   yourself untamed.
In the parts   of you   that have been   tampered with.
        Tell them
                you blamed me.
        Say it louder: speak with full use of your tongue.
        Tell them
        I've been here,
        invisible,   stealing bits of sun   when you're not looking,

        unlearning to hate this body,
        unlearning to hate you,
        unlearning to nurture man   without desperation.

Tell them   this story is ours;   we were stolen;
        and then saturated in griefs;
        the color of crimson; scarlet; ruby red.
Then you buried our truths   the same way you buried my father:

        in the story of your suffering,
        in the story of your faith,
        in the story of your blood,

in the place I never called home;
in a place where God has forgiven;

and your wounds are healed
but where I am shattered
and your blood is my river of red sin.

Prayer II

Today I learned that I'm a sinner
& I can't fathom dying in hell
after poverty & anxiety &
homelessness & never meeting
my father. & I have always been
afraid of hot places and dwellings
without windows or hope. I have
always been afraid. & now I'm
surfing the internet for a cure for
sin. A remedy for dreaming about
a home where I have a bed but
I'm not kneeling to pray; I am
desiring to be touched; to be
romanticized; to be less savaged;
to turn the other cheek; to blink
without crying; to be what my
mother never was; to bleed
enough to break and understand
it.

Truth

is our grandma's silence is a peace that comes when we cannot understand her hurling items   down the hall   & this volcanic pile of smoke and welted wigs was all the noise we needed to feel buried in bodies that
belonged to the history of theft and annihilation. To know insult like God and fear the solitude of what happens after the flood, after the baby is born and not wanted & after not knowing the distinction between night and day but to know the stench of sound & asphalt against our cheeks.

is our mother's verbal passions securing our future. Teaching us to remain marred & leveled with   hatred for love & loyalty. To quest for freedom outside of
maternal bonds by running down the hall   of pity and lapse judgments. To go a lifetime with hurting and see only the thing that hurts. To become an audience of saints that will never reach God. To resist healing. To
revolt against ourselves before dinner each night. To count the stars and not mean it.

is I was never made to sink. I was shaped from the image of God and helium. I
keep my family's history in a photo album down the hall   in a house no one visits. My children are there. I am the kitchen. Inside me there is a stove of secrets where all the women hoard a blaze of men that only brought them fire. Burning never excited me and I never stopped being cautious of silent women or women who never learned to keep their mouths shut.

10 Reasons Why You Refuse to Love Yourself:

"You are terrifying, and strange and beautiful; something not everyone knows how to love" —Warsan Shire

Your mum says: *"love is a waste of time."*
Loving someone who doesn't have a father can be risky.
Your legs housed too many shadows.
You're a sinner.
You're a blemished sacrifice that barely made it over the veil.
No one loves a harlot.
You're a sinner.
Resisting the devil is harder than you thought.
The remnants of rape kiss you as you sit listening to the rain.
Loving yourself is war.

Untitled 5

About this mouth
that kills
midweek; mid-sentence,
tongue lashing,
throat swallowing
dead,
wanted alive
but is well aware
death is inevitable.
That mouth that
licks the thick sweet syrup
off your lips,
and screams "I need you"
as it welcomes a hearty
appetite.
The smutty lipstongue,
that articulates unfinished secrets.
The labial vehicle
that sleep talks,
recites poetry,
sings Psalm 91
in a barbaric tongue,
and burns glass bodies.
This mouth; the treacherous sword,
is oral in its performance
of raw entertainment.
muzzle meter, exotic verbalizer,
filthy, pretty, incinerating torch.
These weighty sacred jaws
is a giftcurse; won't stop
spilling vocabulary vomit.

It wrecks me.
It wrecks me.
It wrecks me.

Church

I sit in the middle row and nod 'cuz the fire is upon us and I am saved from the
torture of others but not yet myself. Africa has placed his continent on my lap
and I am a trivial city, wondering, about the day I will breathe. And then,
again, maybe I should pray. But instead, I grab Africa's hand and
kiss it, 'cuz the fire never burns unless the blood is wiped on
your forehead and you can scream ten "Hallelujah's to
your neighbor while clapping your blessing into
manifestation. I don't belong here, but there
isn't any place in particular that will have
me, so I wipe my tears and swallow
the earth. Nothing is moving
but the fire & only me
and Africa knows
jus' how it
burns.

And

& the person behind the counter is a man

& he reminds me of my father

& he is a gray haired, pretentious, bastard

& he is talking slow and careful

& somehow I have begun to romanticize our meeting

& take him in my closet to dream his shirt off

& he is mine

& we fall apart between spring and summer

& I begin again

& then the man says: "6 dollars and 50 cents"

& I look up

& my father is gone

& I recognize there's something about loving a man who has hurt you

The Burning Bush

I've been in the habit
of writing things that burn
& I imagine one line
at a time,
plus my smoldering voice
against delicate lettering,
so raw, so black, so explosive,
and the little girl,
hiding inside me
peeking out of her hefty body
wondering what kind of woman am I
and what
kind of man loves me
and what kind of America
takes these immolation chants,
and call them freedom,
hell; paradise
or maybe these are single mother scripts
gradually resurrected from the ash
having their way with me
but,
my two sons aren't born yet
and I have yet to form any good feelings
towards careless black men or boys
and so, there are always questions
and then answers
and then silence:

the bush was burning with fire, yet the bush was not consumed (Exodus 3:2)

What I'm writing will not die.

Valley of Dry Bones

For Jonah

I keep having the same dream:

I'm in church   and the ladies are singing,
their notes   tearing the veil
            between
            what's been consecrated   and what was never meant to be.

God keeps telling me

that I must say something

            but
I marry my silence   in a stiff ceremony
where my mouth will not open
            & I'm sinking into the belly of a whale

            facing something incomplete
and irrational

something that keeps me   nomadic

running to a place   where I am not   pretty   or comfortable
running because   I do not believe

running from   relentless arms
running because every year the world is ending

running to a place
where night really does feel this way

and there's a chance I may be   *swallowed.*

I think this is where the dream ends: the ladies are gone,

my mouth identifies a language.
I grow a plant   that later dies

the sun is hot   the ocean defies movement
        the sky is blue   the city is a sound

& the world is not ending

A Vision

We kiss.
Two blurred lines,

meticulous; unhurried
undressing each other

in the part of the city
no one goes.

His mouth
where it ought to be,

my hips; stairs,
and this man climbs

readily, while he
licks his lips

& measures the night
against the woman

who needs him.
& when we finish

peeling the August
afternoon,

we expose a house
full of mirrors and faith.

A place where God is unblinking
& the sun is standing still.

Privacy

Remote women
with prodigies
tugging on their Levi's
lie bare/open
with public atrocities.
They stay awake
each summer night
boiling in mistakes;
clinging to opaque secrets
hanging in their windows.

They're afraid,
of being one step
closer to no where;
from the hotel rooms fuming
in exasperation,
showers of cold water,
and vile faces void of sentiment.

These women,
empty of support,
cover their faces in meetings that
assassinate their character.
Conferences held to question
whether they know
which man fathered their children.

I cling to them.
We remind ourselves
of Jesus's return.
We tell ourselves
He will carry us,
up the dusty four floor walkup.

What will you do when you get out?
She asked

And I answer: *take a bubble bath, while my son sleeps in a bed of his own.*

Acts 17:25

You think you know everything,
like how the earth was formed
and how Adam and Eve coexisted
flanked by each other's delights.

They had it all.

You think you know
whose hands will touch you,
where you will break,
or which poem will
bring you back to order.

You know nothing,

only that tomorrow
will be different
and you dyed your hair last week,
and that your savage needs,
prevent you from wholeness.

You know about the struggles
that dispelled you from the garden,
and that things keep happening
this way,

and that you
are somehow believing
you know more than others,
especially when it comes to being rescued.

But now you're caught
with your favorite dress on
and God is wondering why you are not
living
the way you were born;

naked and hungry
unearthing poems,
and hostilities.

Instead,

you keep touching your broken…

The Prodigal

The man is leaving,
with his eyes   closed
in the middle of the story
where his dreams of being drawn,

            in denim
            in quiet
            in gold

are pulling him away
telling him he can't stay,

            in matrimony
            in insignificance
            in the silence of his body.

He comes upon a strange summer place;
where he can hear his mother   cry
and his faint heart   beat
and his brother tell him   *you're a coward.*

Where the earth
            keeps baring her teeth

            and where he reaches for mourning,
            because the language is simple
            and it tells the rain
            to sing his name   in blood.

Where he has seen colors
fade   into the background

            but he can't touch them.

            Where all of it
            used to make him happy
            but now it is causing him to   retreat

backwards
towards a straight pavement

towards the place he left his memories
towards the place he stretched his mirth
to the place that kept him alive
to the field of his homecoming.

And They Arrived

after Jacob Lawrence's The Migrants Arrived in Great Numbers
(Panel 40 of the Great Migration Series)

singing the blues
weeds;
biting their shins
each step;
enchantment,
each dress, pants, blouse
sketched from the
corners of their fingertips.
And they're arriving,
so late now,
after the rain has passed,
after they have buried
their own
and never believed
this day would come
or that each person
would be a person,
or that each gulp of air
escaping their bellies
would paint the sky
would pave the terrain,
would tell the aching to stop
or begin.
And then they arrive,
when they're revealed
by God
and their sacrifice to
the earth,
which rises to meet them,
in each stride,
in each strand of expectation,
each hue of brown;
leather, flesh and hope,
seeking a beginning,

in an unknown voyage
that begins
the moment they were free to leave…

The Adulterous Woman

I did not come here
    to be beautiful
it's just,
lately I've been
emptying myself

to keep up to give away
what I never had

to salt the wound

    to exist

to love & war
this unshapeliness,

to make tonight special

to smile like I mean it

to catch stones in my palms
    &bleed

to dress my garden
in chocolate cosmos
to disappear into memory…

I came here
    to be salvaged

    to walk on water
unafraid and released

    to hold beauty between my teeth
&tremble
    to lose myself in the smothering crowd

to hear the sweet whisper
of His voice
and find myself forgiven

to go and sin no more.

Genesis 1:3

for Andrew Wyeth's Christina's World

I always wonder why I am here in
the center of ambiguity, placing
parts of myself neatly across the
terrain, bits of sun scaffolding
each bruise and the tears of God
finishing me; marring my flesh
into submissive complexities,
while the sky rages in a decaying
night, garnishing each lonely
space with: Let there be light, and
there was...

Prayer III

If only this heart
        wasn't barbed

and this body   was more
than an anthology   of eulogies

to people   i hate
        but loved   when i knew no better.

        if only my hip broke
like Jacobs's,

        and my prayers
were fervent   like Hannah's,

i would be   more
than a litany of apologies,

        more than the minutes
before the ocean   emptied

itself inside my throat,

        more than a black fence

defending the years i spent
        on my back
worried about the rent:

        Dear God   are you listening?
Wherever you are   i want you to know,

this life is only bearable because
        i am no longer pretending i do not feel alone.

i have longed

to fill this emptiness with cognac

but you have given me   blood.

Valley of Dry Bones

He wraps His arms
    around me,
and transports me
    to a space
where I suck the air
and my bones
    learn to obey.

Brittle bones break,
orphaned bones;
yellow twitching bones

Who levels this valley's terrain?
Who anticipates your ripening flesh?
Who brings life to these bones?

He holds me &
    His grip isn't measured by tears.

These famished bones
    grow full;
these bones of dearth
    are hope.
These raging bones
    are fire bones;
these saddled bones
    will live.

Ode to My Ancestors

Black or Brown

You are Black, or maybe Brown. Your hair nappy. You're youthful and poised; round nose, full lips and thighs as dense as a stack of twenty-dollar bills. You sit on the stoop of a "new building" in the hood and read Baraka, Giovanni and sometimes Shakespeare. The older women pass and slip you a fist full of change telling you to buy an icee from the hairy man who doesn't speak English. Then you grow up and go "home" every weekend to wash your clothes and talk to your black, or maybe brown mum who calls you white. You tell her that Africa isn't a state and the reason she doesn't have wrinkles has nothing to do with placing limes on her eyes but it's the melanin in her skin. You tell her white is a color and not a language, so you can't talk "white". You tell her Bill Clinton was not the first black president and yes you crush on Ben Stiller. Your mum gives you a plate of Cou Cou and flying fish. You appreciate the corn meal and okra parachuting down your throat. The clothes are clean so when you finish eating, you kiss your mum on her cheeks and tell her you're leaving. She offers you a cigarette and questions your honesty when you tell her you quit. Then you notice her shameful tears slithering from the history of her eyes. She accuses you of ignorance, but you hold her anyway and avoid describing your alienation in a world where you were never black or brown just a pariah. Not a Bajan or American, just a fatherless, baby mama without a home. You want to tell her the world never sang your song and the music you invented only lives inside of you, but you grab your laundry and kiss her reminding her you will be back next week. You get on the elevator, dig inside your purse and find your wallet, taking a fist full of change for the black, or maybe brown kids that will be sitting on the stoop...

Hoodie Regrets

for Trayvon Martin

I get up early   and dress   while momma snores   her breaths   cotton
    falling from the moon.

I barely chew my cornflakes   as I get my jacket   & leave   the scent of love
and solace
raising me to be a man   tall and firm   in my hoodie   and ripped Gap denim.

I walk down the street   in a world that isn't mine,   remembering
that momma   told me last night   after dinner   I looked just like
my daddy
    and that was a good thing.

I get to school   people pushing   yelling   tossing their legacies
to and fro   in Jordan's and True Religion's   tarnished with project infirmities
    hiding in their backpacks.

        I am my mother's son   I never belonged here.

I walk to class   the officer stops me   before I reach   homeroom   he pats
my pockets

I take my shoes off   and shake   proving to him   there isn't any   residue
of hatred
from slavery   or war   or the time my daddy was   arrested for
trespassing
    in his own home.

I dust myself off   and go to class   thinking:

        maybe I shouldn't have worn a hoodie

America

for Langston Hughes

I think I may know
a little
about your dreams
deferred
and damaged
turning themselves
around and around
like magic

Cuz' like you
America was never
America to me either

I have imagined what it
would have been like if
this land
which supposedly
is mines and yours
(And everyone else who looks like us)
would've been a land of freedom
or real democracy
and something besides
just a lil' girl's imagination

Oh what a world it would be

But I guess I have some of those basic dreams too
the ones that spin around and around
and kinda go nowhere
and even the ones that seem to play themselves out
unexpectedly

and like you—I wonder:

is there is any land where we are all free

from the emotional and physical entanglement
of a dream deferred?

Cuz' I am too
tangled
stretched and called ugly
but like you,
I won't stop dreaming

You see,
cuz' we never dream in vain
and if we allowed America to defer
our dreams
it would really make me wonder
who is it we are dreaming for anyway?

We the people are the people who hold our own dreams
and they don't always have to be in tears or sorrows

mines are in my legs
cuz' I'm walking with victory

So they can call me ugly
most of the time they can't say it to my face
and even if they did
my America is the dream the dreamers dreamed

and there is nothing ugly about that

Do Not Resist

Two   black men
one uniformed
one in jeans, a tee,
            a torn du-rag
& retro blue Jordan's.

the uniform
            presses against
the tee
& the cotton   retreats.

Four hands against
            a rusting gate.

Sweating brows,
            uttering prayer
masculinity   marr

ed

Someone's phone
            falls to the sidewalk,

Someone screams   *help*

Someone's breathing has braked
Someone's belly growls
            Someone's calling for back-up

& everyone's watching now

even my son
who has nearly finished
            his chocolate milk

            do not resist   says one man

but the other man
        has conquered
 his own black flesh
and breaks free

the uniform runs after him
        but only catches a du-rag

Fallen Stars

for Marcell Dockery

The mattress burned
and you brushed the ashes
in the palms of your youth

as falling embers
drew the shadows
that shaped you.

And as the stars wept
you laughed an impetuous laugh;
charring a glowing night.

Alas, an evening of death
halted your laughter
causing your tears to flow
like blood streaming
from the forehead of Christ.

Who will save you?

Who knows you were just a child
oblivious to death
until they forced you into handcuffs.

And now,
your orange jumpsuit
pulls the pain into my belly.

I couldn't get to you in time.

I crawl into myself;
an anguished mother

Awful Loneliness

I don't wanna hear questions like
What was it like growing up? &
Who is your role model?
or maybe   sometimes
I don't wanna look into the face
of a stranger
and see somebody I know
and suddenly feel heartbreak
and despondency
and awful loneliness...

Sometimes,
I think of a black man
who I really wanted to love
except,
I am a black woman,
whose job is to know love
and see love
but not exactly feel it.
And so,
I don't wanna be the angry aggressive woman
that I am   but I have to be,
and I don't wanna be the emotional scary woman
that I've become   but shouldn't I be?
And then,
it starts to not matter much,
because my grandmother was that way,
and so was my mother,
and it's probably just a phase.
So then,
I'm asked questions like:
Where's your father? &
What does your mother do for a living?
and suddenly,
I'm impotent.
I can't speak
about all the things   too personal

for anyone else to hear.
And so,
I shut off the lamp
and turn down the T.V.
and realize
I'm the only one in the room experiencing
this awful loneliness…

Prayer IV

Our Father…
          teach me how to love
without my body
          bruising
without Noah's flood
          sinking me
into a boat   anchored to glass.

Teach me Lord
to savor
          this martyrdom
like Jeremiah did his tears
          and Elijah with his rain.

Help me Lord
to allow my knees
          to hemorrhage
like the fingers
          of my ancestors
like the foundation of my
          maternal love
like Gethsemane's soil
                    soaked in the tears of Christ,

like my body black
and whole
          in the middle of the universe

stretching   towards iniquity,

blooming
right where you are reaching

for desperate   human needs.

Work Sonnet

A man enters the office. I am the first person he sees
and the first person he walks pass, to get to the white woman
sitting in the hall. The second person he will talk to when the
white woman explains he must see me for answers. As his feet
retreats towards my desk, a violence begins to stir. His apology
knifes resentment into my chest. He is the type of sorry that thinks
It was *too bad Trayvon was the unarmed one or GZ would be dead,*
the type of sorry that needs evidence from a black man that he is an
American, the type of sorry that thinks *its women who are the n-word*
Of the world, the type of sorry that says: *I thought he had a gun*. And
now I'm handing the man a stack of papers, telling him where to sign.
He thanks me without looking into my face. As he leaves the office,
he runs into a friend at the door. They chat. Share a brief laugh and
then his friend walks towards the white woman sitting in the hall.

Waiting for the Morning

The therapist asks: *how do you feel?*
& I feel authenticated
        because
someone wants to know   what it feels like
        to be a black woman who is afraid of the dark

&I keep telling myself to stop feeling   this way
        because my sons are watching
&there is no one else   no one else
        there is no one else

&now I am sitting on the bus
next to a man eating a bagel
&his shirt is torn   and he is calloused
        &I'm thinking of holding his hand,   but he is leaving
& the sun is going down   & gravity becomes God
& God is humid and aching

&now the therapist is asking: *will you be here tomorrow?*
        &I just cry   incapable of explaining
how difficult it is   to anticipate the morning

Ode to My Ancestors

inside my children
there are oceans
hoisting ships of black bodies
their naked backs against the walls.

Each winged shadow of dark
drink the storm
of salt water sweat
& conjure mercies
from age old hymns.

My children play
in these tenacious silhouettes,
recollecting names
we were once told to forget:

Akua, Kwame, Adwoa, Kofi

Legacies paddling murky waters;
and seas of anguish

places my children predict
the little fishies go
when they do not want to be kidnapped.

I tell my children
the waters have history
and aren't just full of tents and toys
built from young boys' imaginations.

I tell them the waters are memories festering
in African cloth and tribal markings
etched on the faces of cargo.

I tell them the waters are memories of home
and grief and memories of death.

But as my children   take hold of regality
          in their kinky twists   and tan armor suits

they disregard
            the bareness of dying hope
 and their ancestors   violent sacrifice

            they play with toys   and pretend to swim
in waters   free

            growing to   become
             shadows   drawn in salt water sweat

            an American Dream,
etched from whispering   waters
                        inside their sweet brown flesh.

Kay Bell can be quoted: "if it makes me cry, sweat, or bleed its worth writing about." She teaches English Composition at the City College of New York and serves as a Student Success Coach at Hostos Community College. As a City College Alumna, she was the college's 2015 recipient of the Esther Unger Poetry Prize and the 2018 co-recipient of the Dortort Prize in Creative Writing for nonfiction. When Kay isn't emphasizing the importance of the rhetorical analysis in her composition class, she is balancing the joy and stresses of motherhood. She lives in the Bronx and is the author of the chapbook: *Cry Sweat Bleed Write* by Lily Poetry Review Books.

www.ingramcontent.com/pod-product-compliance
Lightning Source LLC
LaVergne TN
LVHW051019080826
845145LV00009B/2705

* 9 7 8 1 6 4 6 6 2 3 9 1 4 *